THE A

Canadian born, UK base international business write. She has written more than twenty published books a several joke books, of which the all-time favourite, *The Horse Lover's Joke Book* has been consistently in the top ten category best-sellers since the early 2000s.

Suzan started riding when she was eleven years old and soon joined the Whaddon Chase Pony Club, of which she has very fond memories and to whom she now occasionally offers her help. She is also a committee member of the BRC affiliated Aspley Guise and District Riding Club. She has had to have a few years off riding due to ill health but spends many a weekend writing for dressage judges.

Suzan lives in Bedfordshire with her son, three dogs, and three cats.

The
PONY LOVER'S
JOKE BOOK

The
PONY LOVER'S
JOKE BOOK

Hundreds of laughs for everyone
who loves ponies and everything
to do with them

Suzan St Maur

KENILWORTH PRESS

Text copyright © 2011 Suzan St Maur
Illustrations copyright © 2011 Dianne Breeze

First published in the UK in 2011
by Kenilworth Press, an imprint of Quiller Publishing Ltd

British Library Cataloguing-in-Publication Data
A catalogue record for this book
is available from the British Library

ISBN 978 1 905693 38 2

Illustrations by Dianne Breeze

Designed and typeset by Paul Saunders
Printed in Malta by Gutenberg Press Ltd

Kenilworth Press
An imprint of Quiller Publishing Ltd
Wykey House, Wykey, Shrewsbury, SY4 1JA
Tel: 01939 261616 Fax: 01939 261606
E-mail: info@quillerbooks.com
Website: www.kenilworthpress.co.uk

To the Whaddon Chase Pony Club
…with whom I had so much fun when I was young

★ Equestrian terms revisited

Above The Bit

A polite term describing a pony that throws its head up so high it goes forward with its ears inserted up its rider's nostrils.

Andalusian

A wild, temperamental horse with very small, tight quarters that wears lifts in its shoes and dances about wildly. Useful for DTM provided that flamenco music is played and its rider wears castanets in both hands.

Anglo-Arab

A politically-correct breed of pony or horse that straddles both western and eastern cultures, without once mentioning Afghanistan, Iraq, Barack Obama or Osama Bin Laden.

➜

Behind The Bit

Another polite term describing a pony that not only throws its head up high, but also turns a backward somersault thereby landing its rider in the doo-doo and making an absolute idiot of itself.

Behind The Vertical

A dressage term describing a pony that spends most of the test with its nose between its front feet attempting to buck its rider off.

★ The three (equestrian) bears

Baby bear comes downstairs in his jodhpurs, a clean shirt and his Pony Club tie. He sits in his small chair at the table. He looks into his small bowl. It is empty. 'Who's been eating my porridge?' he squeaks.

Daddy Bear comes downstairs, in his breeches, top boots and pink coat, and sits in his big chair at the table. He looks into his big bowl and it also is empty. 'Who's been eating my porridge?' he roars.

Mummy Bear, in dirty jeans and paddock boots, sticks her head through the serving hatch from the kitchen. 'For Heaven's sake,' she yells, 'how many times do I have to drum this into your stupid heads? It was Mummy Bear who got up at half-past four this morning. It was Mummy Bear who skipped out, fed the horses, groomed them, plaited them up, got the lorry ready, filled the haynets and cleaned the tack. It was Mummy Bear who then came in, woke you up, unloaded the dishwasher from last night and put all the dishes away. It was Mummy Bear who fed the dogs and cats and cleaned out the bird's cage.'

'It was Mummy Bear who then walked the dogs. It was Mummy Bear who fumbled around in the chicken shed to get some fresh eggs. It was Mummy Bear who made the tea and sliced the bread ready for toast. And now that you have been so kind as to drag your bad-tempered backsides down here and grant dear old Mummy Bear an audience, listen carefully as I never want to have to say this again:'

'I HAVEN'T MADE THE BL**DY PORRIDGE YET!'

★ Equestrian terms revisited

Bell Boots
Boots put on a pony that freaks out when the bell is sounded for it to begin its showjumping round, with the boots intended to calm its stress enough to clear the first fence before galloping straight for the exit.

Bloodstock
Horses bred from a long line of successful forbears, but who – like some of the aristocracy – have inherited degenerate attributes like small or non-existent chins, large ears, shrill, whiny voices, large teeth, unbelievably small brains, but the ability to run like h*ll when there's money in it.

Brood Mare
A female pony or horse who by the age of fourteen has bred several foals and has found her way efficiently

→

around the social services system, hence being the proud tenant of a council yard housing all her offspring (all by different stallions of course) in comfort and claiming maximum benefits to educate them all to Olympic level.

Bronco (US)
A savvy old horse who entertains people at rodeos and other shows by kicking up its heels and dropping idiot tourists over its head or shoulder and then goes home to a calm paddock where it snuggles up with a yummy sweet bran mash and its best friend, a small goat.

Cannon Bone
A bone in a pony's leg named after nineteenth century cannons that worked superbly when in good condition but caused endless problems when things went wrong.

★ Roses are red, violets are blue

A senior instructor was giving a showjumping demonstration to a Pony Club audience, using a sturdy Welsh Cob that one of the group had brought along. The Welshie hopped over everything very capably but simply would not go over a rather flimsy upright. Each time the instructor rode him forward, even used her whip, but the Welshie wasn't having any of it.

The PC members glanced nervously at each other, wondering what the instructor was going to do about it ... perhaps lower the fence, or even smack the Welshie harder?

But all the instructor did was to get off the pony, lead him around in a ten metre circle, and whisper in his ear. Then she got back on, set off in canter towards the spooky fence, and the Welshie jumped it perfectly.

After the demonstration the owner of the Welsh Cob boldly went up to the instructor and asked her what she had whispered into the pony's ear. 'I shouldn't really let on my secrets, but as it's your pony I suppose you have the right to know. I recited a little poem: "roses are red, violets are blue – ponies that refuse are made into glue."'

★ Short Snorts

What do you call a Connemara who loves classical music?
A sym-pony

What do you call an Exmoor that's good at business?
A com-pony

What kind of horse wears a sweater, jeans, and cheap boots?
A plainclothes police horse

What time is it when a fat pony sits on the fence?
Time to mend the fence!

What's spotted, stands in a puddle when it rains and doesn't get wet?
An Appaloosa with an umbrella!

★ Whip Round

After spending nearly four hours arguing with officials at the regional department of transport trying to get her new horsebox plated and ready for the road, Amanda's mum was steaming with anger. On their way home, Amanda said they needed a new schooling whip so they stopped at a tack store. They went up to the counter with the chosen whip and the owner said, 'will that be debit, credit card or cash?'

'Cash!' snapped Amanda's mum. Then because she felt guilty about her rudeness, she added, 'Sorry, but I've just spent four hours trying to persuade those idiots that our lorry's paperwork was all correct. I'm about to murder someone...'

'Do you want the whip wrapped?' asked the store owner with a sneaky smile. 'Or are you going back to the department of transport?

★ Why ponies are better than boyfriends

★ Ponies' feet and shoes usually don't smell, unlike a boyfriend's stinky socks and trainers.

★ You can't turn a boyfriend out into the field when you want some peace and quiet.

★ You're not likely to have to put up with a pony's mum, dad, brothers and sisters at Christmas time.

★ Your pony always thinks you look great, even when you haven't straightened your hair.

★ Ponies do not normally play, or watch on TV, football, rugby or other boring sports.

★ Ponies do not need to be entertained by PlayStation, Wii, Xbox or other electronic activities.

★ Your girlfriends won't have any interest in chatting up your pony.

★ Your pony won't get jealous if you take your friend's pony out alone for a hack.

★ Ponies are not interested in shaving their heads or getting tattoos, body piercings, or rings through their earlobes the diameter of the Blackwall Tunnel.

★ If you want to dump a pony, you just sell it or put it out on loan.

★ You won't get upset if your pony forgets to send you a Valentine's card.

★ After you've sold or loaned your pony, you know it won't phone or send you miserable texts at 3 o'clock in the morning.

★ You know your pony would never dump you – well, not in that way, anyway.

★ Ponies' friends are not normally loud and shouty, and don't ignore you.

★ Ponies do not normally get big problems with zits.

★ You'll never have to stand out in the pouring rain to watch your pony play soccer or rugby.

★ Ponies do not play drums or loud guitar music in terrible rock bands.

★ Ponies do not have small, tinny hatchback cars with 900 watts' worth of stereo system blaring.

★ Ponies' stables are not littered with a half-metre depth of empty Coke cans, week-old, mouldy takeaway curry leftovers, school books, laptops and dirty laundry.

★ Why boyfriends are better than ponies

★ Feeding your boyfriend a McDonald's is a lot easier and warmer than trying to tie up a haynet in the dark on a freezing night.

★ If your boyfriend goes lame or gets ill, your parents won't need to pay his vet's bills.

★ If your boyfriend gets tummy ache, you won't need to walk him around and around a chilly yard until the vet gets there.

★ Your boyfriend will usually get someone else to clip his hair, and you don't have to pay for it.

★ Boyfriends are much less likely to mistake your new blonde hair extensions for yummy haylage and so won't be inclined to eat them.

★ Boyfriends don't normally object to getting into a trailer or lorry.

★ Boyfriends are usually (but not always) easier for non-horsey parents to understand.

★ You can communicate with a boyfriend without using more than one or two aids.

★ Boyfriends buy their own shoes, brush their own hair and go to the dentist by themselves.

★ Boyfriends will come indoors out of a muddy, rainy field without you having to go and fetch them.

★ Equestrian terms revisited

Canter

A pace considered normal amongst most horses and ponies, although some Western disciplines dispute that by calling the slow versions of it a 'lope.' Snotty Europeans argue that the 'lope' is merely a lazy four time apology for a canter. Americans argue back that if you Euro-wimps were to spend eight hours a day earning your living in the saddle instead of prancing around for four minutes in a dressage test, you'd appreciate the comfort of the 'lope' too.

Cantle

The back part of the saddle that you hit when despite assuming the jumping position you have misjudged things a bit and your bottom gets walloped as your pony lands. (Serves you right for getting left behind.)

Carriage Horse

A polite term for a horse with unbelievably formal manners that would cheerfully carry a lady across a burbling stream or lay down its New Zealand rug so that she could walk across a muddy gateway without getting her expensive paddock boots wet.

Cart Horse

A derogatory term referring to horses of a certain stature who might not fit into our notions of elegant equestrianism, but who could kick the billy-o out of most show ponies, showjumpers, dressage horses etc. and also show carriage horses a thing or two.

Centre Line
The imaginary trajectory up which we assume many dressage riders must ride despite their minimal chances of getting it straight unless they work to at least medium level or beyond, and then only when they're very lucky.

★ Short Snorts

What's as big as a pony but weighs nothing?
The pony's shadow

PONY OWNER: 'My pony has gone lame. Do you know a good horse vet?'
YARD MANAGER: 'No, all the vets I know are humans!'

How do you tell the difference between a pony and a mouse?
Try picking them up!

What's the difference between a pony and a piece of paper?
You can't make a paper aeroplane out of a pony!

What's the difference between a pony and a banana?
Have you ever tried to peel a pony?

★ Praise the Lord

A vicar wanted to sell his son's pony, and when the first interested party arrived, this young girl's mother asked if she could ride the pony around their paddock to try it before her daughter got on it.

'Of course,' said the vicar. 'However bear in mind the pony responds to religious terms rather than the usual voice aids, but he's very good. If you want him to move on faster, say 'praise the Lord' and if you want him to stop don't say 'whoa,' but instead say 'amen.'

The young girl got on the pony, adjusted her stirrups, checked the girth, then gathered up the reins and said, 'praise the Lord.' Sure enough the pony walked on perfectly. She tried again to see what happened, saying 'praise the Lord' – and the pony trotted on.

After a while in trot she thought she'd try again to see if it still worked, so said 'praise the Lord' and sure enough the pony broke into canter. As they were approaching a nice open space, the woman decided to give it one more go to see what happened.

'Praise the Lord,' she said, and off they went into a flat-out gallop. Suddenly, she realised that they were heading straight for a cliff and a sheer drop. The woman panicked, shouting 'whoa, whoa,' and pulling on the reins, but with no luck – until finally she remembered what to say.

'AMEN!' she shouted and just in the nick of time the pony ground to a halt. The poor woman was so relieved that she just sat there, pushed her helmet back and said, 'phew! Praise the Lord!'

★ Short Snorts

What do you give a pony with a cold?
Cough stirrup!

What animal always goes to bed with its shoes on?
A pony!

What is a pony's favourite sport?
Stable tennis!

Why did the foal cough?
Because he was a little hoarse!

Why was the farmer hopping mad?
Because a pony had trodden on his corn!

★ Etiquette for ponies and horses

Bedding
Your humans will be thrilled to see you wee copiously into the fresh bedding they've just put down in your box; it's an expression of how much you appreciate all their hard work.

Chewing your own environment
After all, it's *your* box. You just chew what you want, where you want, so it's comfortable and inviting.

Dinner manners
To be socially correct you simply must pull all the hay out of your haynet whether you want to eat it or not, especially when you've just had fresh bedding put down so it all mixes

in nicely with that. This provides your human with a refreshing and interesting challenge when they come to skip you out very, very early next morning before they go to work or school.

Doorways

An open door is a fun invitation to get you and your human having a great time! Make sure you exit slowly so he or she thinks there's some hope of catching you, and just as they reach your head ... it's rock and roll time and off you go at a brisk trot! This is a game that can go on for hours. It's even more fun on a really cold, icy day, or when it's raining very hard.

Holes

You can, of course, dig a big hole in your field when you're turned out, but that's a bit boring. It's far more *chic* and sophisticated to dig lots of smaller holes. Even better? Scratch up a bit of earth around each hole so your human thinks it's badgers or rabbits. You really can never have enough holes in your field, so make sure you keep up the digging on a daily basis.

Neighing: don't be put off by the fact it's a cliché

You probably don't watch movies where every horse you see – even if it's dead – has to neigh in the soundtrack just so every viewer knows there's a horse nearby. Anyway, you can use this to your social advantage. Do it – lots – at all hours of the day and night. Your owners will thank you for it as it will draw attention to the fact that there are ponies and horses around, and will reassure them that you're still alive even at four o'clock in the morning. You may even scare off potential tack thieves...who knows!

Nuzzling

Humans love nothing better than to be nuzzled by their beloved pony or horse, especially when you've just had a long drink of water or have been eating your hard feed. And to make it an even better delight for your human? Wait until they come to check you over before they go out for the evening in smart, dressy clothes, and then rub your head all over them as hard as you can. Sweet!

Playing about

If you're out in the field, feeling a bit lively and bucking and galloping around for a laugh, make sure you do it right by one of your human's big horses. That way if you fall over, the big horse will take the impact and he or she will have to be off work for six months – not you! Simple, isn't it?

Snort rules

Snorting – especially when your nose is feeling very runny and stuffy – is something humans just love, particularly when they're in their work clothes, school uniforms or competition riding kit. It's one of your obligations, as their pony or horse, to oblige by snorting over them as much and as often as you can.

Visitors at your home or yard

Although your humans entertain other human visitors, they really don't want them ever to come back again. You can help in this regard by nipping the visitors' hands if they try to feed you, biting their shoulders as they walk past your box, or kicking out at them if they venture out into the field. Easy – and such a valuable asset to your human!

★ Equestrian terms revisited

Chaps

Those strange creatures with whom some girls go out and who occasionally turn out to help us cope with the strains of Pony Club activities. Some are known as 'half-chaps' – they make an effort now and again but only if footie isn't on the telly.

Chukka

An Indian term referring to the casual nature of polo whereby points can be scored by picking the ball up – provided that you have very long arms – and chucking it as hard as you can throw it, so saving your pony a good few hundred yards of painful gallops and your team the inconvenient need to follow you. Can also refer to what riders do due to eating Indian takeaways after shows, as in 'chukka-uppa'.

Clear Round

A showjumping round that means you have cleared all surrounding obstacles including ambient spectators, large and incredibly vulgar sponsors' exhibitions, overflowing beer tents and prize bulls in pens with rings through their noses trying to head-butt anyone who dares to look at them.

Collection

A dressage term referring to the whip-round needed when your PC team has failed to get into the ribbons at a competition and everyone is just dying for a McDonald's.

> **Coloured**
> (archaic) A now politically incorrect term referring to
> a horse or pony's colouring, despite the fact that the
> erstwhile 'coloured' horse describes a very multi-racial
> combination of white with black and/or brown which
> makes a lot more sense than the ways in which we
> describe humans.

★ Well, who said that?

Most days, a young girl would go into the field to fetch her
new pony to go out for a hack. She'd walk up to the pony,
Bingo, and say, 'hiya Bingo! Hope you're feeling well,' catch
him, and then tack him up.

One day, as she was saying the same thing, the pony
turned around and interrupted her. He said, 'ever since you
bought me each time you've come into the field to catch me
you've said, "hiya Bingo! Hope you're feeling well," and I'm
fed up with it, OK? And in any case my name is NOT Bingo,
it's Pokerface.'

And with that the pony wheeled around and galloped off
across the fields.

The girl was so amazed that she could hardly believe it, but
took off after the pony, running as fast as she could. Her collie
dog, Bits, joined in and ran with her. After a couple of miles
the girl was very tired, so she stopped to rest, sitting down in
the long grass and wiping her face with her handkerchief.
Bits, the collie, sat down beside her, tongue lolling.

'You know, Bits, I've never heard a pony speak before,'
said the girl.

'Me neither,' said Bits, puffing loudly.

★ Short Snorts

BREEDER: 'I've lost one of my ponies.'
FRIEND: 'Why don't you put an advert in the paper?'
BREEDER: 'Don't be silly, he can't read!'

What is the difference between a pony and a flea?
A pony can have fleas but a flea can't have ponies!

A girl with a pony on her head went to see the doctor.
The doctor said, 'you know, you really need help.'
'Yes, I do,' said the pony, 'please get this kid off my foot!'

Why are ponies wiser than chickens?
Have you ever heard of Kentucky Fried Ponies?!

What do you get if you cross a polo pony with a
white bear?
A polar-pony

★ Fire away

Matthew and the other members of a Pony Club had just finished a tour of a local fire station, complete with a talk from the senior fire officer about safety, especially where stables and barns are concerned.

But personal safety was high on the agenda, too, so as Matthew was leaving, the fire officer said, 'right, Matthew – can you remember what to do if your clothes catch fire?'

'Yes,' said Matthew proudly, 'I definitely do NOT get dressed in them.'

★ Short Snorts

What is the easy way to get a wild pony?
Get a schooled one and annoy it!

Why is a pony braver than a hen?
Because the pony isn't chicken!

What is worse than raining cats and dogs?
Raining ponies!

How are ponies and hippopotamuses alike?
Neither can play basketball!

What do you call a pony with a carrot in each ear?
Anything you want as he can't hear you!

★ If you crossed a pony with a dog ...

Dales – Labrador: **Dablador**, a pony prone to crib biting on the stable half-door

Exmoor – Spaniel: **Exmaniel**, small pony good at flushing birds out of the bushes

Fell pony – Pitbull: **Fitbell**, a very nasty pony that loves to fight others

Norwegian Fjord – **Retriever**: Rewegian, a nice natured pony whose tail, as well as mane, sticks straight up in the air

New Forest – Newfoundland: **Newflounder**, a pony who can't see the wood for the trees

Icelandic – Husky: **Icesky**, a pony that loves to pull sleds

Hackney – Jack Russell Terrier: **Jackahack**, a pony that's very good at catching rats

Haflinger – Springer: **Hafslinger**, a bouncy pony that only gets tired half the time

Gypsy Vanner – German Shepherd: **Germanner**, a fierce pony with an incurable wanderlust

Highland – Shih Tzu: **HighShihtz**, a pony with unfortunate intestinal issues

Dartmoor – Doberman: **Dobermoor**, a small pony that's very good at guarding prisoners

Falabella – Poodle: **Floodle**, a tiny pony with an incredibly curly mane

Shetland – Rottweiler: **Shrekweiler**, an evil little pony that will scare any intruder away from your tackroom, yard, turnout fields, house, garden, village and probably your whole county as well

Connemara – Cocker Spaniel: **Monnecock**, a strange pony that looks like a car chassis

Welsh – Collie: **Wollie**, a sweet-natured pony that's not very bright

Welsh Cob – Setter: **Wetter**, a large pony that loves hacking out in the rain

Polo pony – Boxer: **Pobolox**, a very rude pony that swears a lot

★ Clever clogs

Two girls were talking over a coffee about their ponies. 'The other day I fell off Jupiter when were out on hack, and really sprained my ankle very badly. And there was no-one else around.'

'So what did you do?' asked the other girl.

'It was amazing – Jupiter got hold of my belt in his mouth, lifted me right up and took me back to the yard.'

'Fantastic!' said the other girl. 'What happened next?'

'He put me down very carefully so I didn't have to take any weight on my bad ankle. Then he went and phoned for help!'

'That's outrageous,' said the other girl. 'Your Jupiter must be the most magical and clever horse in the world.'

'Clever?' sneered the first girl. 'Silly twit only went and phoned the vet.'

★ Equestrian Q & A

How do I get my mare to go into labour?

Go back into the house and lie down for half an hour.

How can I get my pony to really get into an outline and do a super dressage test?

Take him out into the manège when it's getting dark and everyone wants to go home.

How do I cure my pony's constipation?

Load him into a freshly-cleaned trailer.

How can I get my pony to wash his own feet?

Clean out your water trough and fill it up with fresh water.

How can I make sure the weather gets at least ten degrees colder?

Clip your pony and turn him out.

How can I make it rain?

Get out into the field and mow the hay.

How can I get my mare to come into season?

Take her to a showing show.

How can the breeder get my mare in foal at the first attempt?

Tell them to get the wrong stallion out of his box.

How can I make sure my mare gives birth to the perfect foal I've always wanted?

Sell her before she foals.

★ Equestrian terms revisited

Colt
Derived from a US gun brand which uses the same name, this describes a young male pony with attitude described as 'explosive,' and with a substantial amount of fire power in his hind legs especially when the farrier happens to ask him to lift a foot.

Connemara
A romantic breed of Irish pony that loves nothing better than singing 'When Irish Eyes Are Smiling' and sipping a drop of Guinness while trotting along a leafy bridleway.

Counter Canter
A lateral dressage movement performed in a super-market checkout when you manage to skip the

queue and perform leg-yield across to the next checkout without anyone noticing.

Cross Ties (US)
A fancy New York term for the sort of fussy neckwear young American riders wear in a vain attempt to emulate the sophisticated, elegant dressage, show and showjumping gear sported by us incredibly smart and pompous Europeans.

Curry Comb
A favourite amongst the equestrian population in India, the curry comb is a portable device that enables all equestrians who use it to ride for hours at a time without once losing the delightful scents of vindaloo, whether on a hack, in the show ring, during a showjumping round or a dressage test, a flat or steeplechase, or even a game of polo.

★ Cheeky horsetrading

A pony trotted over to an ice cream van one summer afternoon and asked for a choc ice. The owner of the van handed this over to him, and in return the pony gave the man a £10 note. Not unreasonably, the man reckoned the pony wouldn't know much about money, so just handed the pony a £1 coin in change.

'We don't get many ponies here buying ice cream,' smiled the man.

'Well, at £9 for a choc ice,' said the pony, 'I'm not surprised.'

★ Equestrian terms revisited

Cutting Horse

A breed or type of American horse with strong political views and an unbelievably sharp tongue that cheerfully insults not only all forms of equestrian disciplines but also Barack Obama and even George Washington.

Dartmoor

A breed of English pony known for its unnerving fondness for breaking wind far more than other breeds, invariably in the key of 'D'.

Draw Rein

A rein used in training, schooling and other preparatory exercises to ensure the pony has ample opportunity to express itself artistically and benefit from the visual freedom art provides.

Drop Noseband

This is the type of noseband careless riders can use on their mounts as even if you drop it, it will still more or less keep the pony's bridle from falling off and might even stop it opening its mouth too far and getting its tongue over the bit.

Dressage (Adult)

A highly popular equestrian discipline whereby competitors attempt to charm the judges with the latest fashions in designer riding clothes, Christian Louboutin or Jimmy Choo boots, and fascinators designed by Philip Treacy to BHS 3-point safety regulations bearing the code EN13 84 PAS 015.

★ Short Snorts

What kind of ponies live in Antarctica?
Cold ones!

How do you fit five ponies into a car?
Two in the front, two in the back and the other in the glove compartment!

How does a pony get out of a small car?
The same way that it got in!

What do you get if you cross a parrot with a dressage pony?
A pony that can be your test caller as well!

POLICEMAN: 'One of your ponies has been seen chasing a man on a bicycle.'
YARD MANAGER: 'Nonsense, none of our ponies knows how to ride a bicycle!'

★ Spurring into action

A snotty young girl who only rode at weekends on her friends' ponies went into a tack store and said she wanted to buy one spur.

'You what?' said the owner. 'You can't just buy one spur; you can only buy two.'

'Well, that's a cheat,' said the snotty young girl. 'I only need one. After all, if I can get one side of the pony to go faster, the other side has no choice but to follow.'

★ Top 10 Spook Inducers

10. **Paper in the wind** ... this could suffocate us. Don't give us any of this CPR nonsense because we don't believe you can do it, even to fellow humans – never mind ponies.

9. **Yapping dogs** ... you think they're cute. We think they're a nightmare.

8. **Puddles** ... oh, yeah, not very deep? Have you never heard of quicksand?

7. **Wheelie rubbish bins** ... big enough to swallow us whole. Well, OK, maybe just a miniature Shetland.

6. **Babies in prams** ... our foals aren't anything like as noisy, and they don't travel in stupid noisy buggies.

5. **Fancy patterned rugs** ... oh, please. Just how last year are they?

4. **Garden hoses and ropes** ... so we don't have serious snakes in the UK, but we're animals – OK?

3. **Even smaller ponies** ... yuk! They're sooooooo arrogant.

2. **Gale force winds** ... surely you don't need us to explain these ..... whooooooopss!

1. **Tractors, combine harvesters and other clanky farm equipment** ... look, we're not agricultural animals, OK? Forget trying to make us think we're cool with all the noise and smelly fumes. We spook for good reasons, and those are some of them.

★ Short Snorts

Where do you take sick ponies?
To the horsepital!

What is the slowest racehorse in the world?
A clotheshorse!

What has four legs and flies?
A sweaty pony in the summer!

What's a pony's favourite TV soap?
Neigh-bours

Why don't ponies make good dancers?
Because they have two left feet!

What looks white with red spots?
A grey pony with measles!

Why did the pony cross the road?
Because the chicken had taken the day off

What do you call a pony at the North Pole?
Lost!

What's small, nippy, loves tourists' sandwiches and has horns?
A New Forest pony marching band

What has four legs and sixteen wheels?
A pony on roller skates

★ Equestrian terms revisited

Dutch Warmblood

Popular breed of horse known for its eco-friendly ability to perform to high standards wearing wooden shoes. Not recommended, however, for owners whose gardens adjacent to the horse paddock contain large quantities of tulips in spring.

Ewe Neck

Term used to describe the front end of a small horse or pony with an ominously curly coat, a woolly tail and the faintest suspicion of horns emerging roughly at the poll.

Exmoor

A breed of pony born and bred ostensibly in the south-west of England, but with sneaky connections going back to Moorish times which its breeders – perhaps understandably – wish to confine to the dim and distant past.

Falabella

Breed of extremely small horse that's known for its ability to sing along to the chorus of Christmas carols, especially where the lyrics involve him/her singing 'fa la la la la, la la la la,' and looking awfully cute while doing it. NB: becomes surprisingly stroppy if referred to as a 'pony'.

Fault

Four of which happen when some idiot 'rebuilds' a fence after the last competitor has jumped and which now falls down when you jump it, purely because (having been put back together wrongly) it would have fallen down anyway at that precise moment. Of course.

★ Essential pony know-how for non-horsey parents

Much as your child's first pony might look like a fluffy German Shepherd Dog or a very large cat, be warned:

★ A pony looks like a small horse, has a leg at each corner, but has priorities that are very different from those of a GSD, or other breed of dog for that matter

★ The front end can bite and the back end can kick, and, er, smell

★ You'll never housetrain it

★ It will not use a litter tray

★ You can't give it a bed in the kitchen by the Aga

★ You can't make it sleep in a doggy cage, although it will agree to a loose box many times the size of that

★ If you love being surrounded by your pets, it might sleep on your bed – but you will need to seek accommodation elsewhere

★ It will not keep the grass short on your lawn, but will probably eat your bedding plants if it can reach them over the fence

★ It will not be a good guard animal – ponies are wimps

★ It can run (gallop) much faster than a dog

★ It's as strong as an ox and can break out of almost anywhere

★ It will cost you several times what a dog does – in fact probably several times what your child does

★ It cannot travel in the back of a Volvo Estate, even with all the seats folded down

★ It will not catch mice, rats, squirrels and other vermin, but those species will find your pony's accommodation very attractive as they just love its feed stuffs

★ It does not require more than very basic electricity in order to operate efficiently

★ It does not have to be transported to school on a twice-daily basis, although it will need some schooling of its own

★ It is a much safer companion for your child/teenager than school friends who have an interest in booze, cigarettes and drugs, because it doesn't use any of those

★ It is probably not a safer companion for your child/teenager than school friends assuming they don't gallop at 30 m.p.h., buck, rear, and try to drop your child head first on the ground

★ It does not come ready-fitted with seat belts or safety harnesses

★ As its top speed is unlikely to exceed 30 m.p.h. it won't involve your teenager in defending a driver friend who has been speeding

★ It requires quite a lot of expense to live at your home or chosen yard, but does not moan about its need to finance travel to Reading, Glastonbury, Ibiza, Malia or other cool places

★ Unlike teenagers who go to music festivals in the UK, a pony doesn't whinge about living in a muddy field for three days or more

★ And similarly unlike a teenager who goes to muddy, rain-sodden music festivals, it won't come home with a load of filthy laundry

★ Ponies' shoes are expensive, but not quite as expensive as the £150 trainers your child demands. However bear in mind that your child's expensive trainers may last a bit longer than the four to six weeks a pony's shoes do

★ Be prepared to spend a lot of money. Quote from *The Horse Lover's Joke Book* …'how do you make a small fortune out of horses? Start with a large fortune.' Sadly this wasn't a joke; it's true. And ponies cost almost as much

★ Equestrian terms revisited

Fell Pony

A sturdy Mountain and Moorland breed that guarantees to traverse all terrain but does not guarantee that its rider will remain in the saddle, especially when the bridleway ascends or descends slopes of 45 degrees or more in bad weather at temperatures below −20°C.

Flash Noseband

A noseband which cashes in on the current rage for fashion statements comprising utterly outrageous glitter, sparkle, Swarovksi crystals and other bling which riders hope will catch the judges' eyes and divert their attention away from a) a number of fences down or b) a really bad dressage test.

→

Flying Change

The change of leg in canter caused by a very loud, sudden noise occurring just beside the arena, a car alarm going off along H E K, or a bit of unfortunate, very loud feedback on the sound system while the pony crosses X.

Free Walk

A section of many dressage tests whereby the pony is expected to seek the contact in a relaxed manner downwards and forwards and either a) takes it literally and falls asleep thereby dumping its rider in the middle of the arena or b) wanders off beyond the gate and joins all its friends while its rider dreams up an appropriate explanation for an unrehearsed exit.

Freestyle to Music

Dressage to music during which a number of specified movements must be shown, but not in any pre-defined order. These usually include double and triple axels, single and double toe loops, lutz, camel spins, arabesques, sit spins, plus of course throw jumps, the height of which are dependent on the decibel volume of shrieking feedback coming through the loudspeakers.

Gaited Horse

A US term referring to their extraordinary horses which not only do walk, trot, canter and gallop but also can be taught boogie-woogie, jive, quick-step, waltz, rumba, cha-cha, salsa and Ceroc.

Galvayne's Groove
The musical style dating back to the 1950s identified by Henry J Galvayne, the world's first equine dentist, who apart from teaching us how to judge older ponies' ages by their teeth also played bass with Bill Haley and His Comets plus many other great rock 'n' roll bands of the era.

Girth
A device used by largish teenage riders to measure their waistlines before having deducted additional volume caused by the triple cheeseburger off the van at 08:00, the HobNobs in the lorry while everyone else had gone off to watch the cross-country, the large latté in the equestrian centre's pompous new cafeteria, and the huge portion of fish and chips bought on the way home and consumed out of paper packaging, stone cold, after the ponies have been bedded down and tucked up for the night.

Grand Prix
An especially large and heavy dressage trophy awarded to competitors whose enormous warmbloods are capable of carrying riders of fifteen stone or more.

Green
A term that describes eco-friendly young ponies which have been fitted with catalytic converters that neutralise all noxious fumes from their back ends, thereby drastically reducing the emission of harmful gases that cause the holes in the ozone layer.

★ Short Snorts

What do you get when you cross a pony with a peppery vegetable?
Horse-radish

What breed of pony is best at playing pub games?
Dart-more

What breed of pony tends to be clumsy?
Fell

What did the hungry Appaloosa say when he finished his haynet?
That hit the spots!

How do you stop a pony smelling?
Put a peg on its nose!

★ Equestrian terms revisited

Hackamore
A bridle designed by Americans that avoids the need for metal in the horse's mouth, thereby reducing the environmental load created by bit manufacturers and reducing riders' ability to ruin a pony's mouth by letting them play havoc with its nostrils instead.

Hackney pony

A term used to describe a pony whose conformation is rather pedestrian, boring, and has been seen many, many times in the past.

Haflinger

A powerful 4WD/SUV/offroader pony that, despite being pretty small, can out-perform many a larger equid by its sheer determination, strength, grit, ability to charm its enthusiasts with its vibrant chestnut body, its cool, cool flaxen mane and tail, and its ability to pull mud-stuck cars out of rain-soaked showgrounds when all other means have failed.

Half Pass

Ticket given to spectators wishing to attend a UK-based Pony Club three-day-event without paying the full amount considering the fact that they're only interested in watching the competitors make idiots of themselves in the final showjumping phase.

Half Halt

A dressage term referring to the halt made by competitors at the end of their test when the pony stops square, then jiggles about with its feet all over the place and drops a pile of doo-doo before its rider has performed the final salute.

Halter

A miraculous device made from soft material that nonetheless has the strength to stop a spooked pony at full gallop.

★ Not a leg to stand on?

Two Welsh Cob stallions were arguing about who should take best of breed in their Mountain and Moorland Championship. Stallion One said, 'I've got to hand it to you, you're pretty much as handsome as I am. But, my legs are a bit longer than yours. And let's face it, that matters. Our breed really doesn't need to look like big horses on cut-off legs any more, now does it?'

Stallion Two replied, 'well you've got a point there, I suppose. But hang on a minute. I'm standing here on the legs I was born with, but I happen to know you've had thousands' worth of extra training, farriery and all kinds of other stuff to elongate your legs. You may be taller than the breed standard, but your foals won't be. They'll inherit what you were born with – not what vets and farriers have managed to change!'

Stallion One looked ashamed and repentant. 'You're right,' he muttered. 'I stand corrected.'

★ Equestrian terms revisited

Head Collar
Another device, this time made of leather, worn by seven-foot, twenty-stone showground security guards so people can see where their ankles finish and their heads begin.

Hoof Pick
Multi-purpose device similar to a Swiss Army knife, used as a screwdriver, boot cleaner, back scratcher, can

opener, lock picker, wheel brace, nose picker (emergencies only) and, oh yes – to clean out ponies' feet.

Hogged Mane
Style of mane plaiting whereby bunches of mane are tied and curled in a corkscrew fashion similar to the shape of a pig's tail.

Hors Concours
Common mis-spelling of 'horse concourse,' another term for a horse walker.

★ Amusing games for ponies on box rest

Poo in your water game

A fine test of your co-ordination! Horses and ponies everywhere practice this but sadly all too few take it seriously. Approached with a good attitude, however, it's a winner, and ponies are at a distinct advantage as their poo ejector mechanisms are nearer the ground which makes it easier to aim. Suitable targets apart from water buckets include feed bowls and that small pile of hay that gathers under your haynet. Practice regularly until you get your accuracy levels up to perfection!

Wee in your water game

This is a less suitable game for mares, but it's great fun for stallions and geldings! Assuming you have a loose water bucket, first pull it out towards the middle of your box. Practise weeing into it there.

The next time your human refills it and puts it back in the corner, pull it out again – but not so far this time. Repeat until you can wee into the bucket where it's placed by your human. The farther into the corner the better! And don't worry if you kick your bucket over – that can start another new game called 'See How Many Times You Can Get Your Human To Re-do Your Bed.'

Spill your hard feed game

If you're not feeling peckish, this is a real winner! Using your nose and tongue, tip your feed container up and over so the contents fall as far as possible into your bed. Then distribute them as widely as possible, preferably towards the centre of the bed where your wee collects. Give it all a good stir around with your nose and feet, so everything dissolves and makes a lovely sludge. Pellets will dissolve with a bit of effort on your part, but soaked sugar beet is great because it's mushy already. Carrots are a problem though; you'd do better to eat those.

Take up fancy wood carving

Even if most of your box is made of metal, brick, concrete etc. there's nearly always some wood around to give you the chance to express your artistic talents. You've got some fab sharp teeth there – they're like your own personal set of carving chisels, and now's your chance to use them! Don't be too ambitious too quickly though. Start by making single half-moon shapes with a simple bite, and gradually work up to more elaborate designs that really will impress your human and stablemates. If you do a truly good, big job, chances are your human will reward you by replacing what you've done with a whole new, fresh selection of wood so you can start again. By now, you should be thinking up some even fancier ideas for designs!

Dionne Breeze 2010

Hay soaking game

This is a fun game to play with your human, especially if s/he is in a hurry to get to school or work in the morning, or is tired, cold and grumpy on a winter's night after a hard day. When your fresh water and haynet are brought into you, wait until your human has shut the door – then quickly grab a mouthful of hay and dump it into your water. Make enough noise to get your human's attention. Then see how many times you can get him/her to come back in and fish the hay out of your water! Scoring: three times = fair … four times = good … five times = excellent.

The rolling game

When your bed is freshly done get down and roll around, ending up with your legs folded up near one of the walls. Thrash around a lot so your human comes running and nearly has a heart attack because s/he thinks you've got cast. Wait until s/he is really panicking, then get up and have a good laugh. (NB: be careful with this one, because you can really get cast. Best not to play it unless there are several humans around.)

The rolling in poo game

This is a variant on the rolling game, and is especially effective if you're a grey, dun, palomino, or mostly-white coloured pony (although it's fun whatever colour you are). After you've done a night's poos – no cheating now, just what you do normally! – get down and roll. See how much of your body you can cover in poo. Scoring: withers and back = five points ... shoulders and flanks = five points each side ... face and poll = ten points ... mane (right down to your hair roots) = twenty points ... tail and dock = fifteen points.

The mane game

All it takes is some careful rubbing on various parts of your box – and you can achieve the most amazing mane styles! Save your human the trouble of pulling your mane by rubbing most of it off altogether; try to make the finished effect as uneven as possible, as this is what most humans find more attractive. If you prefer a longer look, rub carefully so your mane looks as if it has been back-combed into a beehive do. Or if you just love those romantic dreadlocks, get down and roll in plenty of poo before rubbing. Sensational!

The noise game

This one is best played when there are other horses and ponies on your yard. Wait until several humans are around at feed time and then see who can make the most noise and get fed first. Any noise-making method is acceptable; whinnying, screaming, squealing, banging on a door with your foot, kicking over your water bucket and kicking at the walls of your box, etc. The trick is to make as many of these noises as possible all at the same time. The winner is the horse or pony who gets fed first, as humans will usually start by throwing the feed at the noisiest one. Good luck, and get practising!

★ Short Snorts

LAUREN: 'My homework is really difficult tonight, I have to write an essay on my pony. '
MUM: 'Tell you what – you write in your notebook on the pommel and I'll lunge him slowly. '

What do you call a pony with a machine gun?
Sir!

What does a pony with a machine gun call you?
Anything he likes!

What would happen if a pony sat in front of you at the cinema?
You would miss most of the film!

What was the name of a famous historical pony in France?
Napoleon Pony-parte

★ Signs your dressage needs a bit more work

★ Your 15 metre circle shape reminds the judge that she needs to buy some eggs on her way home.

★ You start with a superb serpentine, but the test says enter down centre line in working trot with halt and salute at G.

★ You avoid sitting trot because it makes your grumbling wisdom tooth hurt.

★ Your pony stretches so far and low in free walk that he decides to have a roll while he's down there.

★ Just as your pony does a nice square halt you accidentally drop your whip and he rears.

★ Your strides in 'medium' trot are not so much 'medium' as 'rare'.

★ Your 'halt at G' ends up with your pony nuzzling the judge's nose.

★ Each time you pass some rustling paper at E you do a transition to working gallop.

★ The judge asks you to clear up and remove the broken arena boards before you exit in walk on a long rein.

★ Your downward transitions finish with you sitting on your pony's ears.

★ Your pony decides the arena boards are in fact cavalletti and exits in working canter at K, straight into the lorry park.

★ All the spectators move back several paces from the rails when they see you enter the arena.

★ Your pony performs most of his working canter on his two hind legs.

★ You get doubly penalised, once for 'use of voice' and again for 'use of loud, vulgar swearing.'

★ Your pony performs perfect square halts when you should be in working trot.

★ In the 'judge's remarks' box you can see:

  ● 'Tidy plaits.' (and nothing else)

  ● 'Pony could have potential.'
    (when in fact he's nineteen years old)

  ● 'Final halt and salute should be performed facing judge.'

  ● 'I must assume this pony has a very big jump.'

  ● 'Airs above the ground are not required in a Prelim test.'

  ● 'Next time please inform your pony that there are no Siberian tigers in the hedge by M-B-F.'

  ● 'Pony needs more impulsion if he is ever to perform paces faster than walk.'

- 'Bucks were well ridden despite not being compulsory movements in this DTM test.'

- 'Have you ever thought of using this pony exclusively for driving?'

- 'Upwards transitions should not require such vigorous use of rider's whip.'

★ Short Snorts

What do you call a pony that's wearing Venetian blinds?
A zebra

What happened to Lady Godiva's mare when it realised she wasn't wearing any clothes?
It made her shy

What has four legs and sees equally well from either end?
A pony with its eyes closed

Why is a racehorse an incredibly strong animal?
Because it can take loads of people for a ride all at the same time

What's the hardest thing you find when you learn to ride a pony?
The ground when you hit it

★ Equestrian terms revisited

Hunter

Any native breed of pony capable of foraging for its own food in the wild, e.g. New Forest ponies, although they tend to prefer a diet of tourists' sandwiches.

Impulsion

What you get from your horse or pony the first time you ride him/her with your spurs on.

Irish Draught

Breed of heavy horse known for its insistence on drinking only organic draught beer. Not known to be a particularly reliable type and is especially prone to stumbling.

Judge

A terrifying multi-headed Hydra that spits flames and hisses at your young horse or pony on his/her first time in a dressage arena.

Jump Off

The final stage of a showjumping competition during which your pony jumps over the straw bales and takes off at full gallop towards the lorry park.

Jumping Order

A stage of competition in which few, if any competitors actually want to come first, especially if it's against the clock.

Jumps
Obstacles in a competition over which both you and your horse or pony, hopefully, should jump in partnership.

Junior
Term used to describe young riders who usually are very talented and so make their older co-competitors look rather stupid.

Lame
Refers to bad, cheesy jokes told by spotty teenage boys at Pony Club parties and BBQs.

Leg Up
Describes rider's position when s/he has just been bucked off and has landed head first in a bramble patch.

★ Who is going to open the gate?

Warmblood: Who needs to open it? Haven't you heard of 'airs above the ground?'!

Thoroughbred: Precisely. Let's just jump it and get on with it.

Anglo-Arab: Yeah, what he said! Na Na Na Na Na Na!

Show Pony: Forget it. I am not taking any chances of messing up my manicure.

Highland Pony: Och, the noo, Jock! I cannae be bothered.

Connemara: Sure, I'm just after tryin' it but it's a tough one, begorrah.

Suffolk Punch: Maybe I can lean on it with my big bum...

New Forest: Let me try – can't be any harder than opening a tourist's picnic basket.

Polo Pony: Wait there – I'll go and get a stick and hit it a few times.

Shetland: What a bunch of wimps! Get out of the way and I'll break stupid thing.

Falabella: Who needs to open it? I can crawl underneath.

Exmoor: Now, now. I'll open it, if someone could help me with my shoes?

Norwegian Fjord: I'd do it, but my mane is too tall and might get damaged.

Dales: Never mind opening it – we'll just storm it and get the whole fence down.

Fell: Stand back! You aren't strong enough to do it. I'll do it. Oh, but what if I break it?

Dartmoor: Let me have a go – where I come from everyone's good at picking locks.

Arab: I'll do it for you. No need to get your knickers in a twist. Peace and love, brothers.

Working Hunter: Oh, shut up and stop arguing. A human will be along in a minute.

Gymkhana Pony: You haven't noticed, of course, that while you lot were piddling about I actually opened the friggin' gate along with two more gates further down. So for Heaven's sake get out of my face!

★ Short Snorts

What's the difference between a Welsh cob and an American Standard Bred?
About 3,000 miles!

What's the difference between a pony and a gooseberry?
A gooseberry is green!

Why do ponies eat raw food?
Because they don't know how to cook!

Why did the pony eat the candle?
For light refreshment!

How can you tell if there is a pony in your dessert?
You get very lumpy ice cream!

★ Equestrian terms revisited

Leg Yield
The total number of pony legs visible at a rally or camp, i.e. number of ponies multiplied by four.

Livery
How parents say they feel when they are obliged to get up at some insane hour of the morning to take their kids to a show or rally, after having had far too much to drink the night before.

Lope
The American name for a type of canter, although the lope is performed with hardly any elevation, on a long rein, in a laid-back, strolling fashion. A bit like everything else in America, really.

Lungeing
A very efficient means of working off a rider's excess energy, whereby the horse spins him or her around in circles until s/he calms down.

M&M
Small, rather sweet breed of native pony with a very rounded appearance; comes in a variety of colours including brown, green, red, blue, yellow and orange.

Mare
Affectionate term for a ditzy, air-headed woman or girl, e.g. 'you silly mare'.

Martingale

Piece of tack normally placed at the front end of a horse or pony to limit its head movements. When placed at the rear of the animal the term reverts to its opposite form, i.e. fartingale.

Medium

A level of dressage in which the tests are designed by a mysterious-looking lady who gazes into a crystal ball.

Ménage

The French word for household (yes, really – not a joke) which English speakers invariably use when they mean *manège*, which is the French word for riding school or arena. (Would you really want to school your horse or pony in the kitchen?)

Morgan Horse
Very fast, sporty but old fashioned breed of pony that makes a lot of noise and can exceed speeds of 120 m.p.h.

★ Short Snorts

You said this pony could jump as high as a two-metre fence, but he can't jump at all.
So ... neither can a fence

What do you get when you cross a bird with a pony?
A horse fly

A girl hacked out on Friday. Three weeks later she hacked back on Friday. Is this possible?
Yes, because the pony's name was Friday

Why did the pony cross the road at a Pony Club rally?
To get to the other ride

What could be the most stroppy, slow horse in the world?
A clothes horse

★ How many horsey types does it take to change a light bulb?

Western Rider: Awww, shucks. That lil' old light bulb's gone, eh? Well, when I've been out riding the range on ma horse all day, herdin' cattle an' stuff, fightin' off the bears and skinin' the rattlesnakes, I come home and y'all wanna waste ma time changin' a friggin' light bulb? I'm gonna go hit the hay now. Y'all in the dark, honey? Then y'all can change it yaself...

Endurance Rider: Light bulb? Light bulb?! Are you out of your mind, bothering me with trivialities when I'm trying to get my horse's unbelievably high pulse/respiration/hydration levels down to something vaguely resembling normal? And after that I have at least another fifty miles to go before I can even contemplate changing a light bulb.

Dressage Rider: Change a light bulb? Are you joking? Do you realise I'm trying to learn an Elementary test right now? And the sun's shining? You'll just have to do it yourself, darling. And kindly polish my patent boots *before* you plait up my horse. Don't forget to wash your hands afterwards.

Event Rider: Wimp! I'd do it right this minute if it weren't for having my broken arm in plaster right up to my shoulder after that fall yesterday, but that has to come off tomorrow because it's the first day of Badminton, so I'll change the light bulb before I leave. Meanwhile don't be so silly – you afraid of the dark? Don't be such a big girl's blouse. Only dressage riders whine about needing lights, anyway.

Showjumper: Who needs light bulbs? And for that matter, who needs lights when the whole equestrian world knows that the sun shines out of my backside? Anyway when I'm in the ring jumping you don't need lights because my brilliance is absolutely blinding.

Farrier: I would gladly change the light bulb for you, but I'm running a bit late today.

Natural Horseman: It's not so much about changing the light bulb as it is about understanding its body language and getting a feel for its aura. You might find that easier if you invest in my online course, 'The Dynamics Of The Alpha Light Bulb' which you can download from my website for just £125. Then you'll see that change of light bulb process need not be a challenge, but a simple, practical activity almost anyone can achieve successfully. (Buy the course before the 1st of next month and get my eBook, *Persuading The Reluctant Light Bulb*, absolutely free!)

Pony Club Mother: Well, of course I would have changed the damned light bulb hours ago, but you wouldn't believe the delays we've had getting here today… there was a twister on the M23 that destroyed seven lorries just in front of us…then some idiot had released a herd of more than two hundred wildebeest all over our carriageway of the M25 … and just when we were desperately hoping we'd still manage to get here slightly before our time so Seraphina and the pony could warm up, this alien space craft landed just by us on the M1 and it took hours before the Police could persuade the little green men to leave so we could all get on our way. Could the judge be a sweetie and slot Seraphina in at the end of the competition? And I expect you can find someone else to change the light bulb.

Teenage (girl) rider: Change a light bulb? Me? When I've already turned the ponies out and washed my hair and painted my nails? You can't be serious! I'm just so upset! How could you?

Teenage (boy) rider: Light bulb? What's that? Oh, yeah, well, I'm on mucking out duty tonight so I'll do it tomorrow, OK. Or the next day. Or next week.

★ Equestrian terms revisited

Movement
One of a series of single activities that a horse or pony performs in a dressage arena, e.g. bowel movement (usually right in front of the judge's table).

Mucking Out
An arduous task you just have to perform once you can no longer excuse the smell in a loose box by referring to it as 'deep litter'.

Mustang
A breed of small, sporty American horse that was much favoured by the late Henry Ford and perpetuated by, amongst others, the Ford Motor Company.

Norwegian Fjord
An intriguing breed of pony-sized horse, usually one of various shades of dun with a dorsal stripe, so named

because its mane sticks straight up in the air to a height of several metres – reminiscent of the sides of a fjord in Norway.

On The Bit
Where your horse or pony should be during a dressage test, rather than being above the bit, behind the bit or totally ignoring the bit as s/he normally does.

On The Flat
How keen showjumpers who can't stand flatwork refer to what should be known as 'dressage training'.

Open
A class of showjumping whereby the entrance to the collecting ring is not closed. Suitable for young or nervous horses and ponies who might decide to run back to their friends halfway through a round.

Overbent
Describes a horse that over-flexes at the poll to the extent that it's sticking its nose up its own backside.

Over reaching
A horse or pony is over reaching when, while competing in a ring or arena, it falls over due to trying to swipe a sandwich out of a spectator's hand.

Oxer
A particularly spooky show jump designed to look like the side view of a rampaging bull.

★ Blatant truths

★ There is no such thing as a barn or yard cat who can't make babies.

★ No-one really notices how well you ride until you fall off in front of them.

★ The least useful horse or pony on your yard will be the one who eats the most, needs shoeing every three weeks and needs the vet about once a fortnight.

★ The more people who are watching, the worse your pony will behave.

★ Your best tack is what your pony will chew on most.

★ Your pony will spend more time chewing up and rolling on the most expensive rug you've bought for him, than any other rug he wears.

★ The tack you like least will never wear out. Nor will your pony's most useless rugs.

★ The pony in your life that you have liked the least, will be the most difficult to loan or sell on.

★ When you're clipping your pony, the blades will go blunt roughly when you're halfway through the job.

★ No matter how careful you are, even when you're walking in from fifty yards beyond your yard, it's enough to make your day clothes dirty.

★ No matter how many ponies you want, if you have the space your equi-head count will multiply to fill every box and every available turnout space.

★ Hoof picks are something you are bound to have forgotten, especially when you need one most.

★ If you fall off your pony, you're bound to land on the bit of your body where you were injured last time.

★ Should you find yourself winning in a competition, think about this – the only way from here on is down.

★ Equestrian terms revisited

Pace

What you all do, up and down, up and down, when your mare is about to foal.

Paint

An American term used to describe piebald and skewbald horses and ponies which have started out as plain black, chestnut or bay but subsequently have had cans of white paint randomly thrown over them.

Passage

A narrow space through which an advanced dressage horse or pony is expected to crawl elegantly, calmly and showing a high degree of collection.

Piaffé

An elaborate advanced dressage movement during which the pony is expected to perform extravagant steps in a tu-tu and satin shoes.

Pirouette

A circular dressage movement which can be performed in walk and in canter. When performed in gallop it is also referred to as 'whipping round and tanking off'.

Polo

A mounted game whereby ponies are expected to jump through fat, rounded white hoops that smell of mint.

Prix St George

A very high-level of dressage which includes compulsory movements in which the horse or pony must swish its tail like a dragon.

Quarter Horse

A cheap breed of small American horse that you can usually pick up at a sale for around 25 cents.

Reining

What American western dressage riders think it's doing in Britain 365 days a year.

★ Short Snorts

What can you conclude if you find a small horse shoe on your walk?
That a pony somewhere is walking around barefoot...

Why did the pony stir his muesli with his foot?
Because he wanted to feel his oats

How do you hire a pony?
Put a brick under all his feet

What did the newbie say after his first pony trek?
'I can't believe something stuffed with grass could be so hard'

Why was the pony charged up?
Because it was haywire

★ Things to say that will make your farrier love you

★ Don't worry, the dogs will stop fighting under your feet if you give them a piece of hoof each.

★ With the amount of money you charge, you should make ME a cup of tea.

★ How come you're driving that old van when you're making so much money?

★ Can you do this mare outdoors? I know it's raining but she hits her head on the ceiling when she rears in her box.

★ I'm just going to feed the other horses and ponies while you're doing that, OK?

★ You can only come in the evening or weekend – I do work, you know.

★ Are you sure you've got those shoes on the correct feet?

★ If that pony wasn't such a vicious kicker, I'd trim his feet myself.

★ While you're here, could you just trim that donkey's feet? He's a rescue, but he's not all that ferocious.

★ Oh, sorry, I forgot you were coming and I've just turned the ponies out.

★ I was reading all about 'natural trimming' on a website yesterday. Is that what you do?

★ She what? That pony's never bitten anyone in her life.

★ He's a lovely ride and so well-mannered. Shame he hates having his feet done.

★ Ah well, there was a dent in your van already. Was that done by a pony kicking, too?

★ Sorry, I should have let you know, but I've got to go out now. Can you come tomorrow?

★ Can you shoe him so he'll do better canter transitions?

★ Have you got some shoes in your van that could make my mare jump higher?

★ Mum forgot to leave your money and she's gone shopping. Can you do her an invoice?

★ Didn't have time to clean all their mud off, I'm afraid.

★ She's not so bad, really – she kicks a lot but usually misses.

★ Mares can be so silly when they're in season, can't they?

★ I got some used horseshoes at a scrap yard yesterday. Can you use them and save us a bit?

★ I know I said just a trim, but could you just quickly stick some shoes on him as well now you're here?

★ My new pony's feet are pretty bad, I'm afraid – last owner's farrier refused to work on him.

★ I can't understand why those shoes are so worn – they've only been on fifteen weeks.

★ I can't make her stand still, but I'm sure you can as you're a professional.

★ Do you want me to get the twitch ready or can you manage without one?

★ It's a good thing you're running late today, or Jasper would have had shoes on when he kicked your knee.

★ That's not how I saw them do it on Blue Peter.

★ Can you make my pony's feet bigger?

★ You don't mind if this group of inner city kids watches you, do you? They've never seen a pony before.

★ Amazing – she kicked our last farrier in exactly the same place.

★ I'll give you my dad's business card – he's an osteopath.

★ He's not leaning on you – he's just giving you a cuddle.

★ I thought as it's such a nice day, you could do them all out in the paddock?

★ Do you want to go into the field and find that shoe she cast? It'll save us buying a new one.

★ If you have any questions you can ring our vet – she'll tell you how to shoe this pony.

★ My daughter's new pony is only 12.2. Will you do his feet at half price?

★ Sorry about that little grey pony – can't understand it, but she hates men.

★ Short Snorts

What do get if you cover your pony in peppermint?
A polo-pony

What do a fat pony and an old-fashioned mattress have in common?
They're both stuffed with hay!

What's wrong with a mare that uses makeup and false eyelashes?
Glam-initis

What's wrong with a pony that's always playful?
Frolic

What looks like half a pony?
The other half

★ Equestrian terms revisited

Run Out
What your horse or pony is just longing to do in the showjumping ring if you forget to keep your leg on.

Saddlebred
An American horse bred specifically with comfort in mind. Breed standard states that its back muscles must be particularly large and cushion-like so removing the need for riders to use a saddle.

Schooling
What young riders' parents say they should be concentrating on at exam time rather than messing about with their ponies.

Selle Français
Literally, 'French salt' – a gourmet form of condiment you can use to cheer up boring burgers at shows. Also can mean 'French saddle,' which is a little like a GP saddle only, being French, it's shaped like a Louis XIV *chaise longue*.

Serpentine
A bending dressage movement usually performed in walk or trot at Novice or Elementary levels, unless there happens to be a grass snake rustling in the bushes beside the arena in which case it's performed in medium or extended gallop.

★ All I need to know about life I learned from my pony

When in doubt, run away as fast as you can.

You can never have too many sweets.

Don't be embarrassed if you pass wind in public.

You simply have to have new shoes every five to six weeks.

Ignore people who try to spur you on, unless you really like them.

Everyone loves a nice, dribbly, slobbery kiss.

Don't trot when you can jog. Don't jog when you can walk. Don't walk when you can stand still.

The perfect day is eating for at least ten hours – then sleeping for the other fourteen.

Eating lots of roughage keeps you healthy.

Good legs and a well-muscled bum will get you places in life.

Big, brown eyes and a soft mouth are also useful.

When you can't get what you want, tread hard on someone's foot.

At stressful times, do a poo.

When faced with something you don't want to do, dig your heels in.

Follow the herd so no-one can pick you to take the blame.

A short, sharp kick on the shin is a great way to get someone's attention.

Make sure you return the love of people who love you – especially if they offer you tasty treats.

★ Short Snorts

What do you get if you cross a show pony with an octopus?
A dressage pony that can walk, trot and canter all at the same time

What sort of horse can survive for long periods under water?
A sea horse

What do you call a pony who is always being negative?
Neigh...

What do young ponies and eggs have in common?
You can't do much with them until they're broken

Why are clouds like riders?
Because they hold the reins...

★ Equestrian terms revisited

Shetland
A tiny, grumpy, hairy, extremely hardy and very cute group of four-legged islands to the north-east of Scotland.

Show Hack
An incredibly conceited equestrian journalist who writes occasionally for *Horse & Hound* and thinks s/he has the right to criticise everyone.

Showjumping
An equestrian discipline in which horse or pony and rider must get around a ring once or twice in the most theatrical way.

Skip out
What most boys and men do when it's time to do the horses/ponies on a cold, rainy evening.

Snaffle
Term used to describe how a greedy pony illicitly eats his/her stable mate's dinner as well as his/her own.

Speed And Endurance
An eventing term that measures a rider's fitness when, having been dumped at the most distant fence on the cross country course, s/he tries to get back to the showground before the horse or pony does.

Sport Horse

A type, rather than a breed, of horse known for its keen sense of humour.

Stallion

An entire male horse or pony with a lot of attitude, who can be recognised instantly by his hairy chest, strong-smelling aftershave and the rather vulgar gold medallion around his neck.

Tack

A term borrowed from the sport of sailing: in this case what devious saddlery thieves do to cover their tracks when fleeing from your yard, where they've just stolen your tack.

Take Off Point

An imaginary, ideal spot shortly before a fence which you know will either be way ahead or way behind where your horse or pony is when s/he actually does take off.

Tennessee Walking Horse

An American breed of horse that for many generations has been made to walk in such a ridiculous and affected manner it has totally forgotten how to trot, canter or gallop.

Trakehner

A German breed of horse which the Germans have cleverly disguised as a fine warmblood, without letting on to us dimwits that *Trakehner* is actually the German for a trekking pony.

→

Transitions

Changes of pace in dressage dictated by the rider.
Also *involuntary transitions*, changes in pace in dressage
dictated by backfiring lorries, galloping loose horses,
escaped sheep in the arena, etc.

Triple Bar

The place to which many fathers and husbands repair
whilst daughters, wives, etc., fiddle about with those
damned horses and ponies.

Trot

The pace between walk and canter, which has much to
answer for in terms of sore muscles and private parts
particularly in the case of novice male riders.

★ Short Snorts

What do you call a pony that never stops complaining?
Nag

What do you call the breed of pony that bores everyone
with his fancy trot?
Hackneyed

What do you call a pony that works as a film extra?
An equid that just does bit parts

What about the overweight kid who took up riding as
weight-losing exercise?
The pony lost 15 kilos in a week

Good news and bad news: good news is your pony came
first in the seventh egg-and-spoon race. The bad news is,
he was competing in the sixth race...

★ Dohhhh...

Two rather unintelligent men bought several ponies at an
auction. For each pony, they paid £100. They then drove to
another auction where they sold all the ponies for exactly
the same amount – £100 each.

When they got back that night they counted out their
money and realised, at long last, that they had exactly the
same amount as they had started out with – no more.

'You see,' shouted one of the men, 'I told you we should
have bought more ponies!'

★ Equestrian terms revisited

Twitch

Old-fashioned device used to tie up a horse's nose so tightly that it wouldn't dare move, hence ensuring its co-operation during teeth rasping, clipping, etc. Fortunately its use is now confined to shutting up very noisy, bolshie small children at shows.

Walk

Demanding dressage pace that requires the rider to keep the horse or pony awake without jogging or shouting to its friends in the warm-up arena.

Walking The Course

What showjumping riders do on their own two feet prior to competitions, desperately hoping their horse or pony does the same but manages to hop over the fences as well.

Walleye

What you get when you're fumbling around in the dark having left it too late to bring the horses in, and thinking you know your way back to the car, you walk purposefully forwards into a brick wall.

Welsh Cob

The largest of the Welsh breeds, the Welsh Cob is so named because its sturdy, arched neck and bl**dy-minded attitude – reminiscent of a grouchy male swan.

★ Short Snorts

How did the Pony Club instructor get more pupils?
She managed to stirrup more interest

Why did the family call their gymkhana pony 'Bad News?'
Because bad news travels fast

Why did they call the pony a really good actor?
Because he loved horseplay

Why do we use the expression 'horse sense?'
Because it's based on stable thinking

Why are horses and ponies considered moderate creatures?
Because they all know how to say 'neigh'

★ Equestrian terms revisited

Welsh Mountain
Where many of the Welsh pony and cob types are to be found, along with sheep, cattle, English holiday-makers and Australian tourists looking for Snowdon in entirely the wrong place.

Western
A chilled style of riding developed by Hollywood movie makers to show off the dubious equestrian talents of actors like John Wayne, Clint Eastwood, etc.

→

Western Dressage
Western *what?*

Working
A speed/attitude of dressage pace which is intended to show off the horse's or pony's abilities as a draught, carriage, farming, trekking and other working form of equid.

Yearling
Twelve-month old child who is due to sit on a pony for the first time

★ Tonight on Pony TV

Desperate Housewives

DESPERATE HORSEWIVES

The story of four women's shameful neglect of household and marital duties in favour of taking their kids to Pony Club events, plus hanging around gossiping on the yard

Strictly Come Dancing

STRICTLY COME JOUSTING

The ultimate equestrian competition where competitors combine the elegance of dressage-to-music with the fun and frolics of good old fashioned medieval rough-and-tumble

Rock Follies

ROCK FILLIES

How a herd of two-year-olds managed to limbo-dance under their fence and escape every night for six months before being discovered.

Silent Witness

SILENT FITNESS

The dark truth about one pony's tough journey from grass fat to fully fit health without producing a single, environmentally-unfriendly windy-pop.

East Enders

BEAST BENDERS

The soap that charts the shocking day-to-day lives of two evil, hard-hearted dressage trainers who wear spurs with rowels the size of cookie cutters and frighten the life out of both their human and equine pupils.

Dragons' Den

DRAGONS' BIN

An exciting competition in which a group of DIY livery owners vie with each other to come up with the best way of catching the giant rat that's forever getting into the feed containers, with a first prize of a year's contract working for Rentokil-Initial.

Top Gear

TOP FEAR

A dice-with-death show that challenges complete equestrian beginners to get on their horse and ponies and attempt riding the Badminton XC course. Survivors get to try driving a rocket-fuelled car on a disused airfield with no questions asked.

Doctor Who

DOCTOR GOO

A futuristic adventure series that explores what some of our current magic equine potions and lotions can really achieve, and how they can turn our horses and ponies into mindless, robotic Daleks

Have I Got News For You

HAVE I GOT SCHMOOZE FOR YOU

A gameshow for farriers, seeing who can outwit the audience and other competitors most with their most grandiose and outlandish remedial farriery gizmos.

Match Of The Day

CATCH OF THE DAY

A whizzy game show whereby six competitors see how quickly they can get a head-collar on the most difficult-to-catch horses and ponies in Britain ... a post-watershed programme with some strong language.

ANTIQUES ROADWORK

A gentle amble down the country lanes by older riders on older horses and ponies who are a little arthritic and couldn't give a damn about competing any more.

The X Factor

THE GXD FACTOR

The ultimate competition for beginner dressage riders and their horses and ponies to see who can actually ride straight from G through X to D without drifting, wavering, bucking, rearing, spooking or otherwise incurring potential criticism from the judge.

Family Fortunes

FAMILY HORSETUNES

The fun game where family teams of riders and trainers compete to see who can produce and perform the most outrageous fancy dress dressage-to-music routine.

Crimewatch

HORSEWATCH

The sharp-shooting programme that vainly tries to identify tack thieves despite their irritating ability to crack tackroom locks and disappear with the goods having avoided the CCTV, Rottweilers, Evil Shetland Ponies, Enraged Livery Owners and all other serious deterrents.

A Touch Of Frost

A TOUCH OF TROTS

The trials and tribulations of an ageing Welsh Cob who hacks out and discovers crime solutions, but only ever in trot ... to the detriment of its criminal opponents who manage to gallop away from the truth ... almost...

Casualty

CASUALTREE

A tribute to saddlers everywhere who work so hard to avoid our need for hospital treatment when our bums are damaged due to poor seating whilst we attempt great things with our horses and ponies.

Blue Peter

BLUE HEATER

How to use your initiative to get the electric heater working in the tackroom on your yard ... creative ideas to get the damned thing lit and avoid cleaning your tack with ice crystals.

The National Lottery

THE NATIONAL TROTTERY

The quiz and game where horse owners throw caution to the wind and drop their weekly wages into a charity, rather than into the hole that feeds their horses for a week or less.

SEX AND THE KITTY

A shocking tale of debauchery and intrigue when Roger the Shetland stallion falls in love with the yard cat.

Never Mind The Buzzcocks

NEVER MIND THE BUZZCR*PS

The quiz show where riders challenge their steeds' ability to remain in perfect control despite the raucous shriek of modern starter buzzers and the consequent temptation (on the horse's or pony's part) to dump a huge pile of poo right in front of the judges' box.

Home And Away

HOME AND FAR AWAY

An ongoing saga of horses and ponies who are genetically
and physically brilliant at jumping out of whatever fencing
you put up and keep you despairing about it ad nauseam.

Neighbours

NEIGH....BORES

The soap that tells the day-to-day story of film-makers and
producers who insist that every time we are shown the image
of a horse or pony in a film or on TV, it has to neigh or
whinny – despite the fact that in real life it would never do
so at that particular time.

Last Of The Summer Wine

LAST OF THE SUMMER WHINNIES

A gentle countryside romp about those early autumn days
when the winter coat is growing through but it's too early
to clip, so making a horse or pony look presentable is a
delightful challenge

The Weakest Link

THE FREAKIEST LINK

The quiz that challenges horsefolks' ability to identify the
most evil-looking bits and other equestrian ironmongery
only by the sound of its creaking when you attempt to apply
it to your horse or pony, or to yourself.

Coronation Street

CORONARY BAND STREET

The thought-provoking soap that asks the key questions
about pedal stability in horses and ponies ... do owners need
to take steps that will revolutionise the equine foot? How is
modern technology affecting the durability of horse shoes?
Will farriers ever turn up on time?

Heartbeat

HORSEBEAT

A nostalgic series that fondly looks back on quaint moments
in equestrian history, like the leaning-back-on-the croup
hunting seat, twitches, tail docking, ferocious curb bits,
hobbling and other delightful traditions.

Hell's Kitchen

HELL'S TACKROOM

A fly-on-the-wall reality series in a typical tackroom the night
before a major competition ... tempers fray, emotions run
high, the metal polish goes missing and a stirrup leather
breaks ... warning: strong language.

What Not To Wear

WHAT NOT TO WEAR ON A HORSE

Exciting equestrian fashion series based on the
(real life!) book of the same name, by Ginny Oakley and
Stephanie Soskin

Allo, Allo

GALOP, GALOP

Comedy series set in 1940s northern France about a herd of Selle Français horses and how they usurp the ridiculous attempts at domination by an arrogant Hanoverian stallion from the moment he arrives on their yard.

I'm A Celebrity, Get Me Out of Here

I'M A DRESSAGE QUEEN, GET ME OUT OF HERE

Reality/survival series where a group of lady Grand Prix level dressage riders are thrown in at the deep end of a cattle ranch in Wyoming and made to ride Western, out on the range, for eight hours a day ... who will survive to the end of series with a sore bum and not a single passage or piaffé?

Absolutely Fabulous

ABSOLUTELY FLATULENT

Light-hearted series that examines the environmental dangers of horse and pony windies compared with the methane output of other species such as cows, sheep, pigs, humans, etc.

One Man And His Dog

ONE BOY AND HIS PONY

A gentle competition held on Dartmoor, where young lads on Dartmoor ponies see who can round up escaped prisoners and get them penned up as quickly and neatly as possible.

Gardener's World

GROOM'S WORLD

Step-by-step guidance on best ways to deal with bedding, cleaning, and various other stable management issues year-round.

Stars In Their Eyes

STUDS IN THEIR SHOES

A lively talent competition for ponies and small horses, whereby contestants must dance about doing 'passage' and 'piaffé' in snowy, icy conditions.

America's Next Top Model

AMERICA'S NEXT TOP MORGAN

Another exciting competition to find the tallest, prettiest and most slender Morgan Horse in the United States.

Monty Python's Flying Circus

MONTY PYTHON'S FLYING DRESSAGE COMPETITION

A hilarious compilation of dressage tests performed by spooky horses and ponies on grass, in the rain, with a gale force wind blowing.

Family Guy

FAMILY SHY

A comedy series where contestants have to try and spook
a herd of New Forest ponies using various noises and
scary objects, while the ponies are busy tucking into some
tourists' picnic.

The Bill

THE NEDDY

Realistic, gritty soap based on the life and times of street
horses and ponies in Australia.

★ Short Snorts

Why did the family call their lazy pony 'Flattery?'
Because he gets you nowhere

'I heard of a vet who accidentally removed a pony's
complete left side.'
'How terrible! What happened to the pony?'
'Well, it's all right now'

'My pony's way of going is rather funny'
'You should enter him for "Britain's Got Talent"'

For how long should people practise veterinary
medicine?
Until they can do it properly

★ Sport horse

A thoroughbred horse turned up at a football club, walked over to the manager and said he wanted to try out as a member of the team. Not surprisingly the manager was fascinated by a talking horse and decided to see where things led.

The horse was brilliant at ball control – with four feet instead of two it was simple for him to keep the ball away from other players and he dribbled it perfectly all around the pitch. When it came to kicking once again the horse was brilliant – using a hind foot for a long kick and a sneaky sideways push with a forefoot to get the ball away from anyone tackling him.

'That's amazing,' said the manager. 'Superb, but now I need to see you run.'

'Run?' said the horse. 'You've got to be joking. If I could run I'd be in Newmarket.'

★ Short Snorts

OWNER: 'Will this ointment cure my pony's skin problem?'
VET: 'Can't say – I don't like to make rash statements'

OWNER (on phone): 'My pony just swallowed my pen. What can I do?'
VET: 'Use a pencil until I get there'

OWNER (on telephone): 'My pony has just eaten a whole roll of film'
VET: 'Let's wait and see what develops'

OWNER: 'How much will it cost me for you to take out my pony's wolf teeth?'
EQUINE DENTIST: 'That'll be £400'
OWNER: '£400? For ten minutes' work?'
Equine dentist: 'If it makes you happier, I can do it really slowly'

One pony to another as they cross in a warm-up arena:
'I don't remember your mane, but your pace looks familiar'

'How is your pony after he swallowed a £10 note?'
'No change so far'